SOCCER

SOCCER

THEORY, TACTICS, AND TECHNIQUE

Alberts Šeibelis

Translated by Elisa Freimane

VANTAGE PRESS
New York

FIRST EDITION

Published by Vantage Press, Inc.
516 West 34th Street, New York, New York 10001

Manufactured in the United States of America
ISBN: 0-533-12830-7

Library of Congress Catalog Card No.: 98-90540

0 9 8 7 6 5 4 3 2 1

In loving memory of my father, Alberts Šeibelis. He gave me the greatest gift a father can give a child, the desire to excel. He taught me to be strong of heart and to stand tall.

—Valija (Waly) Krotenberg

Contents

Alberts Šeibelis—The Great Master of Latvia's Football

More than ninety years have passed since the birth of one of the most outstanding personalities in the sport of Latvia—football player Alberts Šeibelis. Football is a kind of sport where fighting spirit becomes apparent very clearly due to the fact that each of the teams have eleven players on the football field.

Football was very popular in Latvia during the time of the first free state. It was also Alberts Šeibelis' contribution. Thousands of spectators came to watch the play of the central halfback and forward A. Šeibelis. He was paid no less respect and affection than the popular distance walker, Jānis Dalinnš, although it was always emphasized that not an individual, but a cemented and well-disciplined team of eleven players is the true value in football. A. Šeibelis was the most popular Latvian football player, known by adults and kids—by anybody who had at least some knowledge about the game of football. As to football technique in Latvia, nobody could be compared to him. He was even nicknamed "The Fox" since he possessed special wit and ability to take into the football field. A very intelligent football player, Alberts Šeibelis was applauded by thousands who accompanied him throughout his entire long footballer's career. And his career was brilliant, full of blinding attainments. He, who had a delicate stature and red hair, who was given the friendly field nickname "Šimelis" by friends and spectators, who was endlessly worshiped by football fans as their all-time favorite, the most admired, the most respected, and the most outstanding virtuoso of the football game, was granted a lot of epithets. He was recognized by the Finns as the best Baltic technician and tactician, and by the Estonians as "the devil kid" of Latvian football. Mother Nature had endowed him with a special gift of being a footballer.

Alberts Šeibelis was born on 27 December, 1906, in the small town of Sabile, Kurzeme, to the family of a contractor named Oto Šeibelis and his wife, Dora, and given the name of Alberts Zanis. The family moved to Riga in a year.

His father was killed in World War I. After his father's death the mother and the boy moved to Riga, Alberta iela. The boy first saw the round ball around 1914 when he was eight or nine years old. At that time the ball was driven in every free square. One of such squares was in the meadows of Kiegelu iela, where the sports ground of the Christian Youth Union was constructed later. It has been there, where the young sportsmen hardened their strength in ardent fights. Alberts enjoyed passing the ball from behind the goal, where he had first tried to touch the ball with his foot. He had longed to become part of a team. His dream came true in 1916 when he joined the Esplanade team as a full-fledged player. There was no tampering any more. The fighting had been exciting and they had even played with the second string of the famous "Keizarmezs." In 1917 when the boy was eleven years old, he joined the boys' team "Jakor," where such future "stars" as Emils Urbans, brothers Edvins, Rudolfs, Arvids and Oskars Barda, Kurts Strazdinš, and Karlis Bone have played. The team had mostly practiced in Esplanade and in the square behind the national theater. These years in the so-called "Esplanade school" have to be considered as the beginning of Alberts' "career" in sports.

In 1917 the family returned to Sabile. Due to the lack of having a ball, the boy was not able to play football for several years. In 1919 the department of the Latvian Youth Union, along with the sports section, was established in the town. Alberts succeeded in persuading the school superintendent to buy a football and allow them to play. The boy now performed as a real football "specialist" and team coach.

In 1922 Alberts came to Riga again.

The world football gate was opened to Latvia on 29 June, 1922, when the Football Union of Latvia (FUL) was admitted to the International Football Federation (FIFA). The same year Alberts played several games in the team of sports union "Stradnieku sports un Sargs," and also started his studies at the department of mechanics, of the state technical school. He met some of his friends from Esplanade there. Certainly, a school football team was formed right away. In a year, A. Šeibelis and his team won the football competition among schools. During one of the games a referee named Edvins Barda, who was a famous football player, came up to A. Šeibelis after the first half and asked whether he was the same kid "Alberts" who had once played in Esplanade. He praised the boy and urged him to proceed with his mastering of football skills.

When the famous Riga Football Club (RFK) was established in 1923, A. Šeibelis immediately became its member and devoted himself to football with all his heart and soul. The club had the following motto—"Football for footballers—footballers for football." Only those who started to play early could hope for success. Alberts had taken a wide step forward and now played in a solid team—Riga Football Club. Certainly, he only tried the third string first, a little later, the second string. This was where his real career started. Recalling this time, Alberts Šeibelis said: "As beginners we had a rather hard time. Our captain was Osis Barda. Once, when the third string played against 'Unions,' we lost 1 to 3 after the first half and Bārda delivered such a 'sermon' to us that we felt very uneasy afterwards. He threatened 'to break up' the team if we lost the game. . . . It cut me to the heart. Do I really have to leave the football party now when I have just managed to become part of the union's team? The others also were unusually active during the second half. It was unbelievable, but we won the second half 5:0, and the entire game—6:3. I happened to become hero of the day although I had not intended to, and scored 5 goals from 6! That was one of the happiest days in the beginning of my career as a football player. . . . "

Soon after that A. Šeibelis cleared his way to the national team. In predestined 1924 when the Latvian national team returned from the Olympic games in Paris completely defeated, "cleansing" of the old team and searching for new players started. The young A. Šeibelis "was striking to the eyes" of experts. Thus, being only the second-string player in his own club, the youth was included in the national team, filling the position of the famous central forward, Edvins Barda. His first match in the national team was against Finns. He performed the functions of a central forward. The first international game was followed by many others, but none of them has been engraved upon his memory as this first one.

On 20 July, 1926, in Riga, on the field of the Army Sports Club (ASC), A. Šeibelis took part in the first match against Sweden, in which Latvia unexpectedly defeated the world known Swedes 4:1. Goals were scored by A. Tauriņš, K. Strzdinš, A. Pavlovskis and A. Šeibelis, who scored on a penalty. Also in the years to come, he was nearly always entrusted to execute penalties. This year the Football Union of Latvia (FUL) celebrated its fifth anniversary by organizing a large football competition, in which teams representing Riga, Kurzeme and Zemgale took part. In the final, Riga overcame Kurzeme 3:1 and won the competition. The nineteen-year-old Alberts also played on the team of Riga.

The most popular football team of independent Latvia undoubtedly was the "Riga Football Club," which in the years to come produced most of the players for the national team. A. Šeibelis played together with such outstanding masters as Arvids Jurgens, Pauls Sokolovs, Rudolfs Sokolovs, Arturs Timpers, Voldemars Gravelis, Aleksandrs Abrams, Ceslavs Stanciks, Aleksandrs Roge, Emils Urbans, Arkadijs Pavlovs, Arvids Bradinš, Voldemars Plade, Arnolds Taurinš, Kurts Zvirgzdinš, Adolfs Šimanis, Voldemzars Roze, Harijs Fogels, etc. A. Šeibelis became the master of Latvia while playing in this club.

In 1927 an idea was born—to arrange a Baltic state football competition. In autumn of 1928 in Tallinn, three football teams came for the first competition. A. Šeibelis also played in the team of Latvia. The hardest game for him was the game Latvia played against Estonia, which gathered 8,000 spectators. In the middle of the second half due to an excellent pass by A. Šeibelis, A. Taurinš scored a goal with his head. There was still enough time left. In the thick of the fight, the athletic Estonian forward A. Pihlaks, in anger, sent the ball into A. Šeibelis' face from several metres, since he was not able to overcome Šeibelis. A. Šeibelis was carried off the field on the litter. He felt very nervous in the cloak room, not out of pain but concerned whether the Latvians will be able to hold out. After the win A. Šeibelis as the best footballer on the field, was awarded the first Baltic football club, and a wreath made of oak leaves was put on his head. This was the hardest game in A. Šeibelis' football career. He was also recognized as the best football player in the Baltic states.

For three consecutive years the Latvians did not receive the Baltic Cup. And in two of these competitions A. Šeibelis was not part of the national team. After the Baltic Cup competition of 1930 in Vilnius, a big scandal broke out and all the results of previous competitions were annulled. Every third year was the year of the breach. Incomplete competition rules resulted in conflicts. Until 1933, the Latvian national team had lost only once (1931). On 28 August 1932, in Riga, on the sports ground of the Christian Youth Union (CYU), at the opening parade of the resumed Baltic cup competition, A. Šeibelis took an oath. Latvians finished the competition as winners. The best team player again was the captain—Šeibelis. In 1933 the Baltic cup competition failed again. Still, the crisis was overcome and the competition was resumed in 1935.

Every time when A. Šeibelis showed up on the field, spectators welcomed him with applause. The same happened on 30 August, 1936, in Riga, on the sports ground of CYU, when, during the Baltic Cup match between Latvia and Lithuania, before the presence of 7,000 spectators, Alberts scored the critical goal in the forty-fifth minute of the game. The newspaper *Sporta pasaule* wrote: "Well done, Latvian number 11! Well done, Alberts Šeibelis!" The goal scored by Šeibelis in the last minute of the game caused such an ecstasy, that hats, umbrellas, cases, sticks and other things were thrown up into the field. Nobody was really interested whether he would get his property back. Many of them did not get their hats back, they were lost in the mud, trampled underfoot together with the ruins of broken barriers. The crowd almost crushed Šeibelis while crying "hurrah!" Benches and barriers were cracking, ladies were shouting but the most loudest of all was "hurrah!" Colonel J.

Redlihs dropped a glass of water while he was on the stand's roof beside the radio microphone . . . A. Šeibelis was fantastic also in the game against Estonia, when in the thirty-fifth minute his elegant shot reached the goal of the Estonian goalkeeper Tipners. Exultation by 10,000 spectators was tremendous and indescribable, when the Estonians were defeated 2:1. The "old" master Šeibelis was again the focus of attention! The Baltic Cup went to Latvia! Besides, president of the state, Dr. K. Ulmanis, and the highest sports officials were watching the exciting game. This was a bright rebirth of A. Šeibelis, since there had been a weakening in his career in 1935.

Conflicts did not apply to competitions between Latvia, Lithuania and Estonia at a national level and they proceeded without a break till 1940. Latvians played thirty-two games against Estonians, twenty-seven against Lithuanians. A. Šeibelis took part in many of these games.

The thirties were the peak years in A. Šeibelis career. In 1930 A. Šeibelis changed his team and joined the football team "Riga Vanderers." In 1938 the English name of the team was changed to the Latvian—"Rigas Vilki"/"Riga Wolves" (RV). In 1932 the footballers of "Rigas Vilki"—A. Šeibelis, Dregners, A. S. Manis, R. Kundrats, H. Fogels, C. Stanciks, A. Auzinš, Neibergs, E. Beze, Jaunroze, E. Brede, H. Jenihs, and A. Pavlovs became the masters of Riga. On 17 November the same year at the FUL board's meeting both the master of Latvia—"Riga Football Club" and two national team players—A. Šeibelis (RV) and Vladimirs Berziniš (RFC) were honoured. They had played under the national colours of Latvia twenty-nine times. A. Šeibelis was awarded a silver cigarette case. V. Berzinš—a silver watch. Thus unnoticed, A. Šeibelis had become one of the best and most popular football players.

Understanding of the game and technical skills of A.

Šeibelis increased with years. The footballer no longer demonstrated his excellent technique, dribbling the ball by himself but he passed it precisely to partners. Thus, the audience enjoyed less of the nice moments, when he skillfully led the ball around two or three opponents. It was often reproached that his play was theatrical, that he enjoyed playing to the public. The "playmaster" himself, in one of the interviews, disproved these statements: "I do not like to shoot at random. When there is enough time and there is no need to hurry—I search for somebody who is in the most convenient position to be given a pass." What qualities, to his opinion, are necessary to become a good forward? "First, a forward has to manage the ball technique well; secondly—a quick start is needed. Finally, presence of mind is the most important of all." In football he enjoyed being a forward better than acting as a central halfback, or what he did during his last years in the national team. This position, to his opinion, was the hardest one. Up to 1934 he had played in the national team forty-one times, and as the captain of the team had left behind games in Sweden, Poland, Germany, Finland, Estonia, and Lithuania.

In 1934 the sports monthly *Starts* appealed to its readers and football fans for evaluation of the best footballer of Latvia. Public opinion poll started in April and ended in May. The most votes were received by A. Šeibelis—357, he was followed by E. Petersons (RFC)—331, and A. Jurgens (ASC)—72 votes. "Alberts is, and will be the best Baltic technician and tactician. Such playeres as your Alberts Šeibelis cannot be found neither in Estonia nor Lithuania. It would be a waste of time to look for them in the land of lakes, Finland." Such was the Finnish evaluation after the football game between Latvia and Finland in 1934.

"St. George's Day" for football players started in autumn. As the greatest paper sensation came, the news about the most popular footballer, Alberts Šeibelis, who changed from his old club "Rigas Vilki" to the lower league football team "V.Kuzes fabrikas kulturas un sporta biedriba." Great was the gain for V. Kuze's team and painful the strike for "Rigas Vilki," since the captain of their team, the adviser and outstanding master had left. But he left as a friend, not like an enemy because he was offered to form and coach a good football team in Kuze union. In the football season of 1935, V. Kuze's team was a serious candidate for the Riga one league masterteam and transition to the upper league further on. To the team of Kuze also moved his teammate V. Svistunenko, but from CYU—the young and talented footballer J. Vindinš together with M. Grundmanis and A. Leimanis. Now A. Šeibelis changed to employment in "sweetmakers industries" and delivered products manufactured by Kuze to Riga shops with a strong belief, that his new team, which later on stood out as a very disciplined one, would be successful in the future. The key to every success in A. Šeibelis opinion, was football knowledge and discipline.

Success came soon. "A. Šeibelis—brilliant in Kuze team, especially his excellent passes"; "Šeibelis, the eleven, shows outstanding fighting abilities"—such headlines were common to football reviews by *Sporta Pasaule,* with a remark that V. Kuze's team without A. Šeibelis is the same as famous "Austria" of Vienna without its leader Matias Sindelar! Very often the Kuze's footballers were called the Šeibelis boys. He stood out with his technical mastership as usual.

Besides the Riga championships, the Riga Cup also took place. In 1935, on a late autumn day—17 November, in the final "V. Kuze" met with "Rigas Vilki" on the ASC field and won 4:1. The Šeibelis boys gained the cup of Riga.

In the upper league, V. Kuze's team finished the football season of 1936 as the fourth best team in the state! Behind "Olimpija" of Liepaja, ASC and RFC. In all the fourteen games, three footballers from nineteen Kuze players took part—V Svistunenko, A. Šeibelis and A. Ziemelis. A. Šeibelis scored the most goals. He was the best man in the team also in 1937.

Very popular were the football season opening blitz competitions, arranged by the Riga Regional Football Union, which were started on 25 April and proceeded for eleven years, except 1941. Kuze's team, which was "conducted" by A. Šeibelis reached the semifinal, where they lost the game against RFC (2:0).

On 24 March, 1937, at the FUL board's meeting, the chairman, Lieutenant Colonel Juris Redlihs announced that president of the state, Dr. K. Ulmanis had presented a nice (produced by goldsmith K. Jurisons after the sketch by artist E.Vitols) challenge cup for the Latvian cup competition. On 18 September, 1938 at the Latvian Cup competition, "Rigas Vilki" won the final against "Riga Football Club" 3:1. A.Šeibelis scored the penalty and became the first to score a goal in this game.

The everyday life of A. Šeibelis was subjected to football. Special preparation for specific games, in his opinion, was not of much value to a football player. Surely, before every game he had to sleep and rest his fill. He could not eat any stodgy food, even two days before the match he had to turn to lighter food. It goes without saying that he was not allowed to have any alcoholic drinks. That was the way the best footballer of Latvia prepared for the game. But this did not depress the people close to him. In the evening, after the working day and football, two lively daughters—Valija and Biruta—were waiting for the head of the family to come home. According to his daughter Valija Krotenberga, A. Šeibelis was a wonderful father and man. She also had her special role in the football world of her father. Her duty had been to polish her father's football boots. Every time she "polished" the boots she would recite the Lord's prayer, wishing for her father to win the game again. The most important games were watched also by A. Šeibelis' wife and his two daughters. In winter the father spent more time at home, helping his daughters to prepare their homework, especially in mathematics. In winter he had willingly played bandy, had been good at volleyball and billiards.

Within the national team A. Šeibelis on many occasions had fought against different football clubs of Europe: Czech "Trebich DSK," Tallinn's "Kalev," Tllinn's "Sport" (1927), Czech "Prostejob" (1936), Vienna "FAC" and Hungarian "Sceged" (1937), Dutch "Amsterdam Ajax" (1938), and many others. The anniversary came also unnoticed—the fiftieth performance within the national team of Latvia. On 25 June, 1937, before the game against Germany, LFU paid homage to A. Šeibelis and awarded him. The same as Eriks Raisters, he was the best also in this game. The match took place on the ASC football field, was watched by 8,000 spectators and broadcast on Latvia's radio.

In the article "A Few Lovely Words" by sports reporter A. Šmits, devoted to the anniversary, A. Šeibelis expressed some of his ideas about the game of football: "In football, for instance, it is not close enough to master the ball but thinking about the game and going deep into it is strongly necessary. You should escape from such 'sportsmen,' who do not find any deeper and nicer things in sport but only do everything haphazardly. The highest thing a sportsman can reach is to become part of the national team, but one should not be content with it. You should practise more diligently in order to improve your abilities perfectly."

Right after the game against Germany, in July, Latvia played against Romania. This was a drawn game. A. Šeibelis was among the spectators this time. When during the first half Latvian forwards were not lucky at all in shooting the goal the spectators shouted: "Let Šeibelis play!" To the news that A. Šeibelis was not going to take part in the games of the national team any more, spectators responded with great bitterness and dissatisfaction. In 1937, V. Kuze's team lost the leader of their team—A. Šeibelis who, together with A. Ziemelis and V. Šeino would played in "Rigas Vilki" during the next season. In autumn, after it had dropped to the position in the upper league—the "sweetmakers" team ceased to exist.

In 1938 the "star" of A. Šeibelis flashed up anew. After a year's break he was included into the national football team as a reserve for the game against Sweden. That was his fifty-first game. For the first time he also acted as a reporter, reporting information back to the sports paper *Sporta Pasaule* from Sweden about the travel and the game, which took place on June 10 and was drawn (3:3). The same year he first met with Norwegian footballers while taking part in a friendship game, Riga–Oslo, which was a drawn game (1:1), and scored one of the goals.

Also in the game against Poland in September the same year A. Šeibelis was registered as a reserve and still he became a hero of this game. As *Sporta Pasaule* informed—"Our irreplaceable football hero gains success for Latvia in the second half!" Incredible was the end of the football season of Latvia and fantastic was A. Šeibelis' contribution. The final chord was his club team's "Rigas Vilki" win at the cup of the Latvia final.

On 9 February, 1939, at 6 P.M. on the field of the "FUL," a game took place between two teams of the upper league, "Rigas Vilki" and "Hakoah." This game was a homage in honour of A. Šeibelis at the same time, for twenty years he had been devoted to football as an active footballer. The invincible master of the ball had represented the national team of Latvia for fifteen years! Longer than any other player!

In the thirties more than 7 million people in the whole world were playing football (soccer), in Europe—3.5 million, in Latvia—about 2,000. About 370 games of different ranks took place within the season in Latvia. Interest about football was growing from day to day. Wide discussions arose in the sports media about the style and technique of the game. A. Šeibelis also took part in the exchange of opinions. While training himself for fifteen years within the national team under the coaching of five foreign coaches—a Czech, V. Maloczeck; a Hungarian, F. Molnar; and Austrians, K. Kurtz, H. Tandler, and R. Stancel—a wide game experience was accumulated. To his opinion "the Vienna school" with its typical short, low ball passes and tactical maneuver combinations did not seem to succeed in Latvian conditions, because the technique of Latvian footballers was not yet so elegant to play real football of the Vienna pattern. When playing such kind of football, the actions of the forwards and their passes should be very precise. There was lack of good shots. A fair pass in the field was not enough, such a pass was also needed close by the goal. Due to a lack of precise passes by forwards, the expected success at the opponent's goal was not gained. At the beginning of a fast run, far and often inaccurate passes dominated in the football of Latvia. Gradually, the football of Latvia took over "the Vienna school." The technical mastery of A. Šeibelis was a step forward to such a football of the future.

The master wished to express his ideas to the youth in writing, as he had already done in his articles about football in *Sporta Pasaule,* but in a separate edition. In the autumn of 1939, he surprised his football friends. His book, *Football,* was published. The edition was the first original publication in our football literature. A. Šeibelis had not lacked courage to be the first one in taking this important step. The book sums up the experience accumulated during the twenty years on the football field, of this outstanding sportsman. The edition was devoted to the new generation of footballers, to those boys whose dreams were to play the way A. Šeibelis had played.

Nowadays, the book has become a bibliographical rarity because only a few copies have survived throughout the years, and these copies have already been ranked among the original goldies of our sports literature.

Although A. Šeibelis had been the author of many articles and even a book devoted to football, and was fully competent in the matters of football technique and tactics, he still proceed with his education. In March of 1940, together with forty students, he started his studies by courses for football coaches, arranged by the Riga Regional Football Union. Soon after he took over the functions of the national team's coach, substituting for the sick coach of the national team, Karlis Upenieks. No monetary reimbursement was received for coaching the national team or for playing as an amateur on his club "Rigas Vilki."

In 1940, when the national independence of Latvia was lost, the sports organizations, sports unions, and clubs were abolished. In summer, A. Šeibelis still played in his club's team at the autumn football competition, but soon after, he left the active sports and changed to employment in the fire service. He hoped the fireman's uniform will make him nondescript to the new rule. For all that, he was offered a job as a coach in Moscow. He refused to take the job and his name was included on "the black list." Only by hiding did he and his family managed to escape the deportations of 14 June, 1941.

In the spring of 1942, when Riga was already ruled by the Germans, the former football clubs RFC, Riga Sports

Club, VEF, "Auseklis," "Daugavieš," "Olimpija" of Liepaja, "University Sports" (US) etc., were resumed. Also the eleven of "Rigas Vilki" were resumed in the old membership. Together with J. Bebris, A. Simanis, V. Šeino, R. Perkons, brothers Kudrašovs, A. Ziemelis, J. Skadinš, and H. Vitols, A. Šeibelis also returned. On April 25, and 26, after a year's break, a spring blitz competition took place. In the presence of 2,000 spectators the strong team of "Rigas Vilki" unexpectedly lost their game against the "US" team by one goal. Fighting really hard, they managed to win back the position in the upper league, defeating "Daugavieš" 3:1.

In 1943 "Rigas Vilki" already played without their leader. The family of A. Šeibelis spent that summer in Sabile. It was from there, where their refugee pass started. The magic of football was left to the past, as well as sports equipment, regalia, and awards which were left in the motherland. In November, 1944, the family came to Germany, first Schleswig, then Berlin. Later on, their pass led to Thueringen—Rhoneburg, a rather small, quiet mountain village. The family spent several months there until the American troops arrived. The period of "DP" or "displaced persons" camps started. The family of Šeibelis lived in such a camp located about eight kilometers from the town of Gera.

According to the resident of Australia, footballer Mikelis Rubis, in the spring of 1946, when the Latvian Grosshabersdorf and Furth camps were moved to Mertzfelo near Fischbach, A. Šeibelis formed a Latvian football team in Nuremberg. It developed fast. Together with former players of the upper league and the young players that A. Šeibelis had also coached a strong team was formed at the level of the league of Germany. In the summer of 1946, the team had played against different German, Belgian, English, and Polish teams, and even against the Latvian team of Augsburg, which was supplemented with footballers from the whole of Germany. Within the main string such football players like J. Bebris, M. Rubis, F. Laumanis, Hofmanis, Banderovskis, L. Vedejs, A. Šeibelis, Varakajs, Adamsons, R. Perkons, Danilovs, K. Šmits, Putenis, and many others played. The captain of the team, A. Šeibelis had "conducted" distribution of the ball and passes to the forwards. By precisely performed free kicks, close to the penalty box, he had tested the opponent's goalkeepers. A. Šeibelis lived with his family in Mertzfeld, where he was engaged in football and journalism, becoming chief of the sports section of *Dienas Zinas* published by L. Rumaks.

After the years spent in the camps of Germany, A. Šeibelis made up his mind to move to the United States to the state of Arizona due to its salubrious climate, because his wife suffered a lot from rheumatism. In May, 1949, A. Šeibelis and his family arrived in New York from Bremenhayen by ship. They settled down in Tucson, Arizona. His first job had been diging ditches for one dollar an hour. And he had been lucky to get such a job. Later on he was employed as a driver at the St. Mary's Hospital, and as a heat boiler service man. Two years were spent in hard work, with not more than four hours for a night's sleep. Since A. Šeibelis was a good mechanic, he studied through a special technical course and also finished an English language course, which enabled him to get a well-paid job at the engineering company Temp Rite.

In 1966, A. Šeibelis moved from Arizona to Minneapolis, where he was involved for a short period in the local football life, coaching the team "Black Hawk" of Minneapolis, in which a Latvian goalkeeper, V. Vainovskis played. Still, European football was not popular in America. Only very few of the students at the University of Tucson played traditional football against Mexicans. For some time A. Šeibelis coached the boys but American children were more interested in sports that were more popular in the United States.

At age sixty-five A. Šeibelis retired, lived with the family of his daughter Valija, and taught his grandchildren how to play football.

On 12 April, 1972, in San Diego, California the heart of the great master of football suddenly ceased to beat. On 15 April, 1972, a funeral service was conducted and Alberts Šeibelis was buried at the memorial park of Tucson cemetery.

Living in America today are his four grandchildren and six great-grandchildren.

Alberts Šeibelis will always have his special place in the football history of Latvia because his name is connected to great events in its football history; the co-creator of these events has been him, a brilliant individual. Even if he did not succeed in taking part at the world championships and Olympic football competitions, he reached in sports, all the highest peaks and titles possible to be reached in the free state of Latvia between 1918 and 1940—the master of Latvia, the cups of the Baltics, Latvia and Riga winner, the winner of the spring blitz competition and the "best footballer of Latvia." But the greatest award among all has been the love shown by his people.

Here are the words by Valija Krotenberga in memoriam to her father, in the preface to the facsimile edition of the book by A. Šeibelis, *Football—Theory, Tactics, and Technique*:

> With love, in memoriam to my father Alberts Šeibelis. He gave me the greatest gift a father can ever give to his child—the will to surpass. He taught me to be strong in heart and to stand high.

Through this facsimile edition and the short preface of the publishing house Aplis, the Sports Museum of Latvia wishes to open to Latvian readers at home and abroad, one of the most beautiful pages of the history of our football; about the footballer Alberts Šeibelis, about his comrades-in-arms on the football field more than fifty years ago, and showing honour and respect to him as a man and a father.

Introduction

Alberts Šeibelis (1906–1972) won fame as one of Latvia's and the world's best soccer technicians. He was known throughout Europe and was a symbol of good sportsmanship to millions of youngsters. Alberts Šeibelis was born in Sabile, Latvia, one of the three Baltic states of Europe. He spent most of his childhood in Sabile and in Riga, the capital city of Latvia, and attended the Riga Technical School. Alberts devoted his spare time to his first love—soccer. At the age of seventeen, he represented Latvia for the first time in international games. He was a participant on Latvia's national team fifty-eight times.

The redheaded, somewhat fragile, Sabile-Latvia-born Šimelis, as he was called, was Latvia's best soccer ball technician. He sometimes liked to play little tricks on the field—teasing the referee and calling loudly to his teammates and opponents. For these reasons, Alberts got himself into trouble more than once. Even with all this, Šeibelis was always a threat to every opponent at every moment. He was also the first of Latvia's all-star team to wear the national team's uniform for the fiftieth time. That happened on July 25, 1937 in Riga, Latvia in a match against Germany. If the talk turned to unforgettable moments in Latvian sports, these moments were often a result of Šeibelis' work. No one who has seen him on the soccer field can forget him. Latvians would say that his game sense made Alberts the Fox

("Lapsa") of the Riga Wolf team, and he was just such a fox on Latvia's national team.

Alberts Šeibelis scored goals that were often made in such uncommon situations and were gained so acrobatically, that it is doubtful that he could repeat any of them a second time, no matter how much he might have wanted to. But once-in-a-lifetime achievements are not even meant to be repeated. Alberts is the most prominent Latvian technician of all time, though his tactics are no less noteworthy. Technical skill was what allowed "Šimelis" to pass the ball with complete precision, and only model technique made the delicate redheaded Šeibelis into a powerful goal kicker.

Alberts Šeibelis was a virtuoso in the world of Latvian soccer. Alberts Šeibelis said, "Soccer is a team sport. The score is a reflection of how well the team plays. If the team has a few stars, then on the day when they play well, the other players follow their enthusiasm."

The first Baltic national championships were in 1928. The Estonian-Latvian game in the Tallinn stadium started the tournament. There was no score in the first forty-five minutes. The same occurred in the first twenty minutes of the second half. Then the Latvian's center halfback, Alberts Šeibelis, managed to pass the ball precisely to the attack's right side, which the player headed into the Estonian goal. The score, 1-0 for Latvia!

Enthusiastically, the Latvian team once again pushed Estonia onto its own side of the field. The large Estonian inner wing was angry that he couldn't get past Šeibelis, who was playing one of the best games of his soccer career. Nastily, the Estonian wing drove the ball straight at Šeibelis from a few meters away, and Šeibelis had to be carried off the field. There were only ten minutes left until the end of the game.

Alberts Šeibelis lay in the locker room. He forgot his

great pain and attentively listened to what was happening in the field. Would the Estonians regain what they had lost? To Alberts Šeibelis those ten minutes seemed like an eternity. At last the referee's whistle blew. Latvia had won, 1-0. The Latvian players ran into the locker room, took their captain onto their arms, and carried him back onto the field. There, Šeibelis was decorated with a large oak leaf wreath, and he was given the first Baltic soccer cup.

In 1949 Alberts Šeibelis settled in Tucson, Arizona, in the United States with his wife, Leontina, and daughters Waly and Ruth. He helped raise his grandchildren Albert, Ruthie, Marshall, and Henry in the spirit of sports and love. Alberts Šeibelis has always been an inspiration to young athletes in Europe and America.

SOCCER

A Short History of the Game of Soccer

Several types of games with balls have been played since ancient times. The "discovery" of soccer is divided between England, France, and Italy.

Perhaps the game traveled in ancient times—through Caesar's Roman Legions to Britain—in the same way as in modern times Britain's sailors and merchants have spread it throughout the world. The playing of the game is recorded in Britain in 1350, when their king, Edward III, allowed the people to forgo the study of warfare. Other kings, on the other hand, tried to suppress soccer, but unsuccessfully. Though such ancient games were called soccer, they had little in common with today's game.

Ancient soccer balls were often approximately one meter in circumference. The rules of the game were simple—and often dependent on the particular game's events. Most often one village's men and boys would battle against the same number of men and boys from another village. This game's, or contest's goal was to get the ball, one to two meters in circumference, into a notable place in the neighboring village: into the town hall, the town well, etc. These contests often lasted several days, and, besides that, the lack of rules often led the participants to play in a very unsportsmanlike manner.

The game developed slowly. The ball and the playing field became smaller, the number of players stabilized, and rules were adopted. In 1838, the first soccer rules appeared.

These rules provided for twenty to thirty players on each side, and they forbade players from holding opponents' belts, or standing in the backfield, but with a different meaning than we know now. The flow of the game was left to three referees. Each team supplied one referee, but the third, called the head referee, was chosen by both teams together.

Several decades passed while the game took a form known for the past seventy-five years. As the game changed, the rules were expanded and became similar to today's rules. A deciding step was the creation of the English soccer league. In the league's seventy-five years of existence, the sport of soccer has developed and grown so far that it can certainly be considered a more refined sport.

The History of Soccer in Latvia

Here in Latvia, as in other lands, soccer was brought by English immigrants. Soccer was found in Riga before World War I. It was played by English immigrants who attracted young men to the game. The English even created a team, called Britannia. As more and more young men became interested in the game, and so that competition could be fostered, the Latvians created their own team, the Amateurs. This was the first Latvian soccer team, and it still exists today. Slowly more teams were created. At the start of World War I, the teams dissolved and players scattered. However, many young boys were seen in city parks kicking around soccer balls.

At the end of the war, soccer teams started to meet and organize. The older teams resumed activity and new teams were created. In order to carry out a planned soccer tournament, in 1921 a few dedicated sportsmen, among them the then LSA (Latvian Soccer Association) president, Lieutenant Colonel J. Redlichs, founded the Latvian Soccer Association. From this moment, soccer was on an upswing, improving in quality and quantity. Soccer expanded into the provinces where clubs and state leagues were founded. Tournaments were organized in all areas of the country. International championship tournaments followed, the first with Estonia. Other countries' teams visited us and we traveled outside our country's borders.

Therefore, as soccer has slowly developed, we can happily state that we have greatly advanced in this sport, which is also evident by the large number of spectators at important games. This proves that much has been done on the soccer front, but much must still be done. This sport with its great progress has captivated thousands of people, and our soccer stadiums, though not ideal, have been shown to be too small to accommodate the large flood of spectators. We can hope that in the future this problem will be solved.

The regular battle for the Latvian championship was started in 1922 and up to the present time, the Latvian soccer champions have been:

1. 1922—Kaiservald
2. 1923—Kaiservald
3. 1924—RFK
4. 1925—RFK
5. 1926—RFK
6. 1927—Olimpija
7. 1928—Olimpija
8. 1929—Olimpija
9. 1930—RFK
10. 1931—RFK
11. 1932—ASK
12. 1933—Olimpija
13. 1934—RFK
14. 1935—RFK
15. 1936—Olimpija
16. 1937/38—Olimpija

In the beginning the championship tournament order was such that teams within each state (Vidzeme, Latgale, Zemgale, Kurzeme, and Riga) would play each other and a state champion would be decided. Afterwards, the state champions would decide the national title in a single elimination tournament. This was changed starting in 1927 when a master league or major league was formed, which consisted of eight of Latvia's best teams, regardless of their states, that fought against each other for the national championship in two round-robin sets (twice per season).

This system is still in operation today; only the championship game period has been changed from spring-fall to a fall-spring "season." Previously, the championship season started in the spring and ended in the fall, but since 1937, the first round is held in the fall and the second round after the winter break—in the spring. Therefore, the winner is decided only in the summer of the next year. Now the soccer season's starting date is no longer January 1st, but August 1st.

Soccer Theory

Soccer is an art, and every art has its theoretical basis. So too, in the game of soccer, one cannot lose touch with theory; however, one must be warned not to overemphasize the study of theory or theoretical philosophy. Theory shouldn't be an invented fantasy, and it can't be in conflict with the truth. Opposition between theory and practice really does not exist, because correct theory is created from experience and knowledge. At any rate, common sense will also create a theory that reflects practice and experience.

Theory examines the game itself, the players, and the given situation from many different perspectives. It teaches us how to use different methods of play, depending on the situation in the field, and which method is most suited to the situation. Theory creates strategy, which, in turn, gives players certain basic rules to use in the game. The variations in soccer play do not allow players to use these rules as absolutes, but encourage them to think. Then the player who has some technical talent will, with experience, find a good solution to every problem.

Lessons in strategy are only part of theory, though an important part. Everything else, for example, technique, training, body building, etc., requires theory. Since the game of soccer is a practical art, the most significant elements are those that occur on the field. In this game, a good lesson to be learned is that of criticism. It brings theory closer to life and conditions the consciousness to a more spiritual perception of the game. Criticism is guided by good theory. Theory is the critic's measure, that which fixes for him the course of the game. Of course, criticism must be constructive.

Every soccer player must immerse himself in theory. It is understandable that only technique along with tactics will give good results. The player who hates theory is usually the one who needs it the most.

Theory is the greatest joining force of any soccer team. If the soccer team has a fairly even perception and opinion of itself, only then will it really be represented by the word "team."

The word "strategy" in soccer is taken from military terminology, in which it means the course of battle. Soccer is also a battle, which has its own strategy. If technique gives the body an advantage in the game, then strategy gives the mind ideas that must be used in the battle. Soccer has two types of tactics, one offensive, the other defensive.

Plays help the tactical game. The word "play" (combination) comes from Latin and means "working together" (teamwork). In soccer the word "play" should not be understood only as the ball being passed from one player to another (offensively), because other means of cooperation on the soccer field, even without a ball, are called plays.

For example: 1) if a team's players cooperate so that a player goes after one of his opponents (or tries to take away the ball) and the other team members cover the other opponents, then that is already a play; 2) if both fullbacks—one to the front and one back—position themselves in the field, that too is a play; 3) if, with the opponent attacking, the halfback covers the wing forward and the fullback covers the inner forward—then here too we see a play (defensive tactics). Therefore, a play is defined as the entire team's players' combined tactical cooperation.

In the past in soccer, the word "play" was unknown to us and was also not used in the game. We knew only to kick forward (toward the opponent's goal) and run, or control the ball until an opponent took it away, or, in the best of circumstances, an attempt at the opponent's goal was made. That was called a "solo game."

For this reason, players who did not have decent hits, quick runs, good ball control skills, and breakaway kicks, were not considered good soccer players. Of course, even today the skills mentioned are necessary for every soccer player, but along with these come plays (strategic plays).

In Latvia we have seen many first-class foreign soccer teams, for example: the Vienna "Austria," "WAC," and others. It must be said that we could and did learn from their passing and plays. From this information alone, we can deduce that until about 1930 the foreigners beat us easily, but afterwards we were strong in our game and advanced greatly, and for this reason, the famous professional players did not find their job easy when playing against us. A few tied and even lost to us.

I consider our transition year from primitive to modern soccer to have been 1924. As an example from soccer history, I will mention the Riga soccer club of 1924. In that year one could observe the difference between the club's I and II teams. Team I still played fairly primitive soccer at that time but Team II, on the other hand, tried to use plays in their game. In that same autumn, in the club's internal competition, Team I beat Team II by just one goal. This proves that offensive and defensive plays give much greater advantages.

What sort of advantages do they give? The most important thing in soccer is to get the greatest number of goals possible. This can be done only when tactically correct combination plays are used. Tactics without technique are impossible. The success of plays is dependent on the technique and the proper positioning of the players. Proper positioning means the player always places himself in the field so that he is not covered by an opponent, and so that teammates can easily pass him the ball.

In the ideal game the ball would travel from player to player in all directions without stopping. The ball can be passed without stopping only: 1) if a teammate is open, or; 2) if the receiving player is confident of his teammate's position in advance. I say—in advance! That means that in the game one must be careful and must also think. A player receiving the ball must, in a moment, already know where best to pass without holding the ball. This kind of immediate passing gives the game speed (develops tempo), and also the team with the ball (offense) does not tire itself out as much in taking positions as does the opponent whose assignment is to take the ball away.

If in this kind of game an attempt would be made to get closer to the opponent's goal, where a quick and unexpected hit to the goal would follow, then success would be inevitable.

Strategy for Forwards

As I said before, the most important thing in soccer is to get more goals, but in order to do that, one must be close to the opponent's goal as often as possible. In order to really get closer to the opponent's goal, a productive combination of plays must be used.

Usually an attack is begun by the wing forwards, because their area of play (the part of the field in which they are found) is wider and they are covered less by the opponents. The wings, as well as the other forwards, often happen to be met and hindered by an opponent as they receive the ball, which hampers passing the ball. The best thing to do here would be to make a short pass back to a halfback, who then could pass to an open forward, in this way beginning the attack anew. Frequently passing the ball backward is not recommended. This wastes time and creates less of a chance to score a goal (unproductive play).

Our wings make a great error when they dribble down the sidelines to the corner and then make a high pass centering the ball near the goal. This occurs when they have passed all obstacles and no one opposes them (in a solo play). The wings, if not hindered by an opponent, must attempt to take the ball toward the opponent's goal by the closest and shortest route.

If the wing is running with the ball by the closest route to the goal, then the teammate next to him must immediately take his position. This play is called a switch. There is another way to switch wings. We have often heard our team players shouting "veco" (pronounced vet-swua = the old one). If the right wing has the ball and the inside right forward or center forward shouts "veco," the wing knows that he must pass parallel to the sideline past the opponent and then must switch places with the teammate who has gone ahead to receive the ball. The same thing can be done on the left side, which is then called a left-wing switch.

This kind of switch can be done not only with the wings, but it is also recommended for inside forwards, halfbacks, and fullbacks.

Our wings are often at fault in passing and centering the ball. They kick either behind the goal or into the hands of the goalie. It must be said that a well-passed ball from a wing often results in a goal. For this reason, it is better to pass the ball farther from the opponent's goal, at best near the 11-meter penalty spot.

A forward does not always have to pass to his teammate to the right or left. If players are battling for the ball on one side of the field, naturally the opponent will give all his attention to the side where this battle is taking place and will also turn to that side. In that case, the wing on the opposite side will be wide open and not covered by an opponent.

A very good strategic maneuver, for example, is: if the battle is on the left side, the left inner forward, having received the ball, instead of giving the ball to the left wing or center forward, makes an unexpected long pass to the right wing, who is then free to go for the goal. The same thing can be done from the other side. Not only the forwards, but the halfbacks as well can take the ball to the opposite side. This kind of moving of the game from one side of the field to the other makes it possible, as I said before, to quickly close in on the opponent's goal, from which position an immediate shot at the goal follows without delay.

Not even a second can be wasted when shooting at the goal. The player closest to the opponent's goal, if unable to shoot, passes the ball to an open teammate, who must shoot the ball into the opponent's goal without pausing.

Unnecessary passing close to the goal does no good for the attacking team. This kind of unnecessary play close to the goal could be seen in the 1936 season in the Riga "Vanderer" and "Hakoah" teams. The result was that both teams played beautifully, but did not score and finished low in the championship standings. On the other hand, the "Olimpija" team from Liepaja did not play beautifully, but they played an aggressive game, in which it was important to score. They won the Latvian championship title several times.

Delaying when kicking a goal gives the opponent a chance to pull back its players and, therefore, protect its goal from a score. For this reason, I will say again that there can be no delaying close to the goal, not to mention the penalty area. All of the forwards, especially the inner trio (center, inner right, inner left), must have no unnecessary passing or delaying in the penalty area—they must have only one thought—shoot a goal!

Defense for Forwards

When the team is on the offensive, that is, when it is playing on the other team's side of the field, then the halfbacks must move with the forwards and must try to correct every one of the forwards' mistakes or misdirections of the ball by moving the ball back in the direction of the opponent's goal.

When the opponent is attacking, the halfback must try to upset the attack. Not only the halfbacks, but also the forwards must move back to help the defense. The wings and center forward do not need to do this, but the inner forwards do (from here on, I will call them the inner right and inner left). The wings must be ready at any moment to receive a pass and to take it quickly to the opponent's side.

The center forward must paralyze the center halfback, and he cannot allow him to coordinate the attack, that is, to receive and pass the ball without pressure. The center forward must also be sure that if the wings receive the ball, he is ready to move with them toward the opponent's goal. A situation in which the inner forwards stay on the opponent's side and do not participate in the defense cannot occur. In this situation, the team is divided between forwards and defense. So that this does not occur, the inner forwards, in forming the team's defensive attack, must come to the aid of the halfbacks—they must become halfbacks, but the halfbacks must become fullbacks. Therefore, the inner forwards must be in the offense as well as in the defense.

The Halfback

There are two wing halfbacks and one center halfback. Their job is the most difficult. It is difficult to describe in theory. Depending on the current game situation, the halfback is part of the offense as well as a supporter of the defense. In a word, halfbacks are the team's links. Just as a train has wagons, between which are links, which sometimes pull and sometimes brake, so the halfbacks sometimes drive their own forwards ahead, sometimes slowing the opponent's forwards.

An excellent halfback must have very good technique and strategy, and also must be in good condition. He must also have a good feel for the direction the ball will take, so that he can reach it before his opponent. The ability to head the ball cannot be forgotten, as the halfback uses this move more than other players. The wing halfbacks will perform their jobs satisfactorily only if they get along well with their teammates, especially with the fullbacks and the center halfback. The wing halfback fights with the fullback on his side against the opponent's wing attack. If the opponent's wing attacks, the halfback as well as the fullbacks must be clear as to who does what. A situation may not occur (though it often does on our national teams, not to mention other teams) in which two members of one team repeatedly attack one and the same opponent. For example, if the halfback is going after the inner forward, the fullback must watch for (cover) the opponent's wing.

There are several ways of communicating, which, when properly implemented, will hinder the progress of the opponent's attack. The wing halfbacks and the center halfback should communicate well, especially in those instances when the opponent attacks with all three inner forwards.

This concludes a short summary of the wing halfback's defensive play. We cannot forget that the wing halfback is also an offensive player. He forms an offensive triangle with the wing ahead of him. The main responsibility for the halfback on offense is passing the ball to the forwards. In order to do this precisely and productively, he must survey the entire field and the status of both teams, because the ball must be received by the player in the best position. It often occurs that the halfback works as a sixth forward or goes into the attack by switching positions with one of the forwards. In this situation, the halfback must not forget that as soon as he has finished his job in the attack, he must return to his position immediately.

Usually when the halfback goes on the attack, he moves more toward the inside of the field to increase pressure on the opponent's goal. There can also be a situation in which, for example, the wing forward, having received the ball, is covered by the opponent and cannot pass the ball toward the goal (centering). In this case, the halfback must be right behind the wing forward who passes back to the halfback, who centers the ball.

I would like to describe a situation that might be of use to players as well as team or club coaches.

Two teams are playing—A against B. Team B's best forward manages to get by Team A's left halfback and center the ball, resulting in a score. At halftime, one of Team A's coaches comes into the locker room and starts to yell at his left halfback about not covering the opponent's wing forward.

In the second half, the halfback is never more than a step away from the wing and follows him like a shadow. I must comment that this is the wrong way to cover an opponent. Certainly, the forward will be unable to do anything in this situation, but the halfback could just as well not be on the field. If one forward is missing, the game still goes on, but not so if one of the halfbacks is missing. Another thing that the halfback must do excellently: is to throw the ball in well from the sidelines. A good throw-in means giving the ball to the teammate in the best position. The throw-in must be as precise as a pass from a kick. It is also good if a halfback can throw the ball far into the field.

The Center Halfback

The center halfback is the leader of the team. The team's success is dependent on him. He is the axis around which, for the most part, the entire battle circles. The center halfback is the director whose wishes must be followed by the forwards. A player of especially outstanding ability, who is very talented in technique and strategy, must play this position. He must be in very good condition, because he spends almost the entire game running. If the team attacks, he must move with the forwards to support them.

When the opponent attacks, the center halfback must confuse this attack. The center halfback may not delay in passing the ball. A good center halfback must always survey the situation in the entire field, so that he can always pass to the teammate in the best position. He must be wary of unnecessary dribbling, which wastes energy and much time. It is not recommended that the center halfback play far back in the field; rather, he should play more to the front, so that he can confuse the opponent's attack at the very beginning.

It has been said that a good offense is the best defense, and in this case, the center halfback must remember that he cannot become so enthusiastic about the attack that once the opponent starts his attack, the halfback cannot return to his position in time. The center halfback must be fast so that he is always in position in time. Our team's center halfbacks, even on the national teams, are often heard complaining that it is difficult for them to fight alone against three inner forwards. This sometimes is the case, and here the fault lies with our team's inner forwards.

As I said earlier, when the opponent attacks, the inner forwards must help the center halfback. Then he will not have to fight one against three.

The center halfback, as all other players, must get along well with his teammates. As much as possible, the center halfback should receive all shots out of the opponent's goal, or the fullback should receive them, so that the opponent is delayed in getting to the ball.

A great advantage for the center halfback is his stature and strength. For the most part, men of large stature are seen in this position. There are, of course, exceptions. Many center halfbacks must receive and head balls, and here the tallest will have an advantage. The center halfback must attempt to block all high balls, which come from blocks in the goal, throw-ins, and corner kicks. If the opponent is attacking or kicking a corner kick, then the center halfback must cover the center forward especially well. The center halfback is supported in play not only by the inner and wing forwards, but also by the fullbacks.

The Fullback

A team has two fullbacks—the right and the left. Both fullbacks and the goalie compose the team's defense. The fullback, and especially the goalie, are the last obstacles that must be overcome in order to gain a goal. The players who play in the defense, along with all the characteristics of a good attacker, also must be very composed and be especially good tacticians. They must be very careful and must think quickly, so that they know in a moment what to do—try to take away the ball from the opponent, hinder him from passing to another player, or allow him to take a shot at the goal. A good fullback must notice the opponent's every intention before it is carried out. Not even a hundredth of a second can be lost, so that the opponent cannot carry out his intentions. The fullback must understand each occurring situation and must know what to do with the ball at every moment.

Usually the fullbacks, on receiving the ball, make long and often indefinite forward kicks. This is good if the forwards get to the ball. However, often the ball reaches the forward at the same time as an opponent, or even the opponent exclusively. For this reason, the fullback is advised not to kick far, but to try to pass the ball to an open teammate. If an opponent hinders the fullback from passing the ball, and there is no other choice but to kick a long, forward kick, then the fullback must always try to pass the ball to the wings.

The fullback does not have to take all the balls that come toward the goal; on the contrary, many can be let go, so that the goalie takes them, especially in those cases when an opponent is close to the fullback. In order to protect the goalie from the opponent's attack, the fullback must cover the opponent; that is, he must not let the opponent go by him. Here many a fullback makes a big mistake: while covering the opponent, he turns his back to him. **Every player, not only the fullback, but the others as well, must remember that when covering the opponent, that is, not allowing him to take part in the game, the player must always be facing him.**

Because much of the fullback's activity takes place, for the most part, in the penalty area, where even the smallest violation results in an 11-meter penalty shot, he must guard himself from penalties. The fullback can easily make a violation if he tries to hinder the opponent with illegal moves. Slowing the opponent and hindering his forward motion by use of the body is allowed in soccer, and this is especially important for the fullbacks, but as I already said, in the legal manner. It is not legal, for example, to hold the opponent with a hand, or to put a foot in front of the opponent in order to make him fall. The opponent may be pushed or blocked with the shoulders and chest. Players earn many penalties not because they purposely use illegal moves, but because they do not know how to play within the prescribed set of rules. So the appropriate kind of body play may be more successful, physical strength is also important. That is why we most often see strong and well-developed men in the fullback positions.

Of course there are also exceptions. The fullback is forced to take high balls, such as from corner kicks, penalty kicks and centering with the head, in which case height is very important. When approaching an opponent, the fullback must always try to stay on the inside of the field and must force the opponent to the outside, that is, toward the sidelines, because the goal will be much less threatened from the side than from the center. If the opponent throws the ball in from the sideline, then the fullback must be careful not to stand too close to the thrower.

Sometimes the thrower throws the ball over the head of the fullback, in this way, passing the ball to his teammate. Then, by the time the fullback turns around, the opponent is gone with the ball. A good fullback always tries to keep the ball in the field. It often happens that the ball is rolling toward the end line, and the fullback does not have the time to stop it, turn toward the field and make a shot, but he must make the shot while running after the ball—that is; he must turn the ball into the field. This is very important in order to avoid a close duel, especially close to the goal, in situations when the opponent is running right behind the ball. The fullbacks may never position themselves in a straight line on the field.

As I said before, the forwards must have an understanding with the halfbacks, the halfbacks with the fullbacks, the fullbacks with the goalie. Not only in that order, but in general, every player must have an understanding with every teammate, whether he is in front of him, or to the side, or behind. If the team attacks, the halfbacks go with the forwards, and the fullbacks can't just stay in the back, so that there is an empty space between the halfbacks and fullbacks. The fullbacks must remember that only one, not both, moves forward, and the other stays back, and the one farther from the goal is always the one on whose side play is occurring. If play moves from one side to the other, then the fullbacks must also change their positions on the field. Throughout the match, the fullbacks must keep an eye on the game, follow the game, and move along with the game attack.

The Goalie

The last obstacle to the scoring of a goal is the goalie. The goalie, as the name describes, is the player who does not participate in open play on the field, but who stays in the goal and guards it. The goalie is differentiated from the others by his uniform and manner of play. He is the only player on the team who is allowed to catch the ball with his hands; however, he cannot carry it, and he can hold it only in the boundaries of the penalty area. The goalie, as all the other players, must be a good tactical player who starts well, and who can make good predictions. Besides that, he must be especially composed and confident when catching the ball. Whenever possible, he must try to catch the ball in his hands, or, if the opponent hinders him, punch it into the field. He must guard himself from stopping or kicking the ball with his feet, except in cases in which it is no longer possible to do anything else.

Usually a taller and stronger player is chosen for the goalie's position. That is because he must often catch high balls, not only those that come toward the goal, but also those that go beyond it. If the goalie is short, and the opponent's forwards tall, then the goalie will have a hard time fishing out high balls. For this reason, the goalie, along with the usual kinds of team practice, must practice high jumping and long jumping from a standing position and on the run, and a bit of shotput won't hurt him. Usually taller people are less coordinated. If the goalie is tall and catches high balls well, but low balls poorly, then things will not go well. No matter whether he is short or tall, every goalie must train more in his weak areas.

Proper positioning and stance in the goal are important for the goalie. He must always try to decrease the area of the goal artificially, especially if the opponent attacks from one or the other side. The goalie must always move closer to the goalpost on the side from which the shot at the goal is expected. Then the area of the goal will naturally decrease. If the shot is expected from the middle, then the goalie must be in the middle.

The goalie does not always have to stay in the goal and wait for the shot. If the opponent has gotten by everyone, and the goalie sees that none of the defenders can stop him, the goalie must move (start) toward the opponent without pause and must try to take the ball before the opponent has managed to complete the shot. In this case, if the opponent's shot is successful, then the ball will most often hit the goalie or go into the net. In general, the goalie must make these runs outside the goal precise and in situations with a good chance of success, so that he is always the winner in the contest with the opponent. If, along with all these good characteristics he also has a bit of luck, which is necessary for any good goalie, then he will be ideal.

A Few Words about Practice

A soccer game lasts ninety minutes. In this time the work the players accomplish is tremendous. Depending on the flow of the game, except for a few moments, the team members must be in constant motion. Those who aren't handling the ball must take over another position, attack an opponent, or cover him. This constant movement, with or without the ball, is a systematic physical and mental battle for both teams.

So that the player's physique does not overexert itself, it must be gradually conditioned to carry out this kind of soccer contest. It is not enough to just play in the games to condition the physique (keep in shape), but between games the body must be kept active, kept in training.

Next to the physical job, which is most noticeable to spectators, the players' mental activity is of great importance. Individual players must fit in with the team, with teammates, and must understand each other and work together.

In its long existence, the game of soccer has developed greatly, and the manner of play is becoming increasingly more refined.

It is not possible to learn all that is contained in a first-class soccer game on one's own. A big role is played by a person's natural development and by talent, which, in one and another instance, first-class soccer players are born with. But talent alone is not enough. In order for one to become a good soccer player, there must be great interest in (love for) the game. It is not possible to satisfy all the requirements set by a first-class soccer game without special preparation.

All that is entailed in preparation is called training.

The first thing required of every good soccer player is conditioning. In sports, conditioning is understood to be maintaining the body's fitness (stamina). It is often said that there is good and bad conditioning. Conditioning training is such that with a proper lifestyle—for example, food, rest, work, cleansing the body etc.—the body's capacity for work is increased.

The players' education will be more clearly understood if the art of soccer is divided as follows:

the school of running
the school of the ball
tactics
body conditioning (fitness training)
body care (showering, massage, etc.)

Along with all of this comes theory, which improves the practical work.

Technique and tactics are inseparable things. However, every moment of the game can be analyzed from a technical as well as a tactical standpoint. The mental side of the game belongs to tactics, and it can be said that tactics direct technique. However, it is not to be said that technique is less important than tactics. A first-class game requires a good level of technical and tactical preparedness from each player. With the word "technician," we refer to the kind of player who knows how to handle the ball deftly, even to the point of acrobatics. Of course, a tactician must also be prepared, to a certain extent, to control the ball, but this is not so obvious, because the player's worth is expressed in his intelligent play. If technique is lacking, then the best of tactical ideas cannot be realized. The higher class of players usually combine in themselves both tactics and technique, and other good qualities.

Tactics, as I said, are an expression of intelligence, but in soccer they are usually less developed than the preparedness of the body. As a result, the tactician's greater value can be seen. Every soccer team is kept together by tactics. For that reason, it is also understandable that in choosing players for responsible positions, tacticians have an advantage, and that team leaders must have high tactical qualities. The team's cooperation is based on ideas. Technique is what helps to realize these dreams.

Ball Technique

In order to start to move the ball, it must be touched with the foot; a hit must be made. If the player runs with the ball in the field for a time, and with short, easy kicks drives the ball ahead of him, he is doing what in soccer is called dribbling. In dribbling, the inside and outside of the foot can be used. A play is a planned for moving the ball from one player to another. When making a short pass at a short distance, the inside or outside of the foot is always used. It is different at a greater distance, for example, when a fullback passes to a wing or when a wing halfback changes sides, moving the ball from his side to the other wing's side. In that case, the top of the foot is usually used [this is called "blati," pronounced "bla-tee" in Latvian].

If the goal of the kick is the opponent's goal, then it is called a goal shot. It is often said that a player who can shoot at the goal cleanly and well has a healthy shot. Shooting cleanly and well at the goal is, in a way, a great art.

Our body works according to physiological and mechanical rules. The game of soccer is unique in that the feet are used both for running and playing the ball at the same time. It is different in other kinds of sports. In the wink of an eye, when working with the ball in soccer, all the weight of the body is moved to one foot and supported, and the other foot moves the ball. Let's call one foot the supporting foot and the other the playing foot. Of great importance to the supporting foot is support itself, so that the body can be placed in the correct position in relation to the ball. The playing foot must hit the ball precisely and in time.

The ball can be hit at the center or off-center as necessary. When hitting it off-center, it gains a chance to spin and does not go straight, but takes a curve.

It goes without saying that the upper body, as well as the arms, must work together with the feet.

A straight hit means hitting the ball with the top of the foot ("blati") while pointing the toes down. Usually these kicks are used for longer distances. Every soccer player must know how to perform this kick. Beginners usually make mistakes by incorrectly balancing on the supporting foot and the result is that the kick is unsuccessful, and they even cause themselves pain. By training gradually, the art of cleanly and strongly hitting the ball is acquired. Straight hits can be made low or high. When a shot at the goal must be made, one must always try to make it low. The fullback, when repulsing a ball or a wing passing it to the center, on the other hand, must try to lift it high. The correct execution of the hit is, for the most part, dependent on the state of the supporting foot. When making a low shot, the supporting foot must be slightly ahead of the ball or right next to it. Once the ball is in front of the supporting foot, a high kick will always result. A good soccer player must be competent in all the variations of the straight hit.

Volleying the ball. By receiving the ball directly from the air and moving it farther without stopping, a kick called a "volley" is created. Since our Latvian "soccer dictionary" is not rich in terms, then I will use some non-Latvian words.

Volleyed balls have the advantage of being very quick and sharp, if only they go in the generally correct direction. For forwards shooting at the goal, as well as fullbacks deflecting the ball, volleyed balls are very important. A ball shot in the air toward the goal can rarely be caught. If an air ball is hit at the moment it bounces from the ground, then the shot is called a half-volley. This kind of shot is very difficult, because it is dependent on hitting the ball at the correct moment. It is especially hard to make this shot go low.

Passing

Giving the ball to one's teammate no longer means just kicking. Here a sensitive hitting of the ball—one could say pushing—must be used in such a way that it is easier for the teammate to receive the ball. The ball cannot be passed too strongly, or too weakly. When passing the ball precisely, the inside of the foot is usually used. It can also be done with the outside of the foot, which confuses the opponent. When carrying out plays in a game, both the inside and the outside of the foot must be used, which has a great tactical meaning.

A toe kick is seldom seen in good play. It is sharp and strong, but completely unpredictable. This kick usually occurs when mixing up the opponent's plays and unexpectedly catching the opponent's passes. It is completely incorrect to use the toe kick for free kicks, penalty kicks, corners, etc.

The heel. The ball is usually kicked with the heel by the weakest players because the results can make them happy. If this kick is even slightly successful, which rarely happens, the spectators become enthusiastic and applaud. I recommend refraining from kicking with the heel, because players must try to always keep their eyes on the ball (controlling it), which is often lacking in this kind of trick.

A double kick is called "scissors." The player makes this kick while jumping, and the ball is kicked with the foot that leaves the ground last. The scissor kick is used by the fullbacks once in a while. A player can also do well without it. A big mistake is made when a player, not being hindered by anyone, still makes a scissor kick. It should only be done when being hindered by the opponent, not in every play.

Low and high passes are used in every competition. In a good soccer game, the ball is held close to the ground as much as possible. It has been practically shown that the low pass is much more valuable than the high one. With that I'm not saying that one can get by with only low passes, and that it is always possible to play only that way. If one team is playing a high, and the second team a low game, then the second team must know how to get to high balls. In the battle, situations occur in which it would be a mistake to stay with a schematically low game. This must be said especially about passes at a long distance. At a greater distance, an opponent will often be found in a position to intercept the ball. Here a half high pass—over the head of the opponent to the teammate—would be appropriate. From all this we see that good teams prefer a low game, using the high one when necessary.

Heading the ball. We have ascertained that in soccer not only does it happen by chance, but often a high game is used on purpose. Then heading is very important. When playing with the head, the tempo of the game is increased.

Instead of waiting for the ball to come to the foot, it can be sent onward with the head. If the opponent is expecting a high ball, in order to stop it with his feet and then continue playing it low, he can be surprised by your heading the ball.

As we see, heading has several tactical advantages; however, it would be incorrect to exaggerate this play. If at all possible, the ball must be stopped with the foot in order to continue a low game. Quite often in a contest, one player happens to take the ball with his foot, the opponent, on the other hand, with his head. It can be deduced that heading is most often used in a close battle which is why it is important to develop this play.

The ball can be stopped, as well as hit, with the head. When the ball is coming high from a greater distance, it can be directed with the head noticeably far, and sharply. It is possible to hit the ball with all the parts of the head. Hitting the ball with the top of the head can cause pain to the player and is unpredictable; the most precisely directed heading is with the forehead. A forehead hit has the advantage that the ball always stays right before the eyes, and besides that, the head cannot be hurt in this way. With the forehead the ball can be hit not only forward, but also to the side. It is important to make the hit with the head while jumping. The hit must be made at the moment during the jump when the body is farthest from the ground and at its highest point, or before then. The ball should never be hit when the body is already falling back to the ground. In that case, the hit will no longer be successful, and though stopping of the ball will occur, that can be done without the exertion of jumping.

When hitting the ball with the head while jumping, especially when hitting to the side, good body control is needed. The player who jumps first when heading has the advantage of finding himself above the others, and he can turn his upper body in the necessary direction. The others, on the other hand, hinder each other when jumping, and in making contact with someone already jumping, a player can easily lose his balance. It is incorrect to jump too early, because then when the ball comes, the body will already be falling back. Developing good heading skills does not mean just hitting the ball away somewhere, but hitting it so that it has force and direction.

Much training is required in order to be able to head the ball to another teammate's feet or to hit correctly into the goal.

From a standing position, jumping for the ball is done with both feet, but when running—with one foot. The arms are usually thrown out to the sides, which helps the body control its balance and helps it turn while in the air. Much care must be taken to keep the arm motions correct and within the parameters of the rules. The arms may not be used to push an opponent nor to support oneself on an opponent. By training gradually, one learns to hit the ball with the side of the head or even the back of the head. I would like to emphasize once again that an effort must be made to learn this skill, though it is enough to have a good command of hitting with only the forehead.

Stopping the ball is the beginning and end of the game of soccer. Even if a soccer player plays first-class soccer for ten or more years, it is vital that he practice stopping the ball at every training session. A training session with the ball without practicing stopping is unthinkable. Never will a player have reached such a level of preparedness that improvement in this regard would be unnecessary.

The majority of players stop the ball with the sole of the foot. This method had possibly existed since the birth of soccer, and it is not bad in one or another instance, even today, but not always. If the opponent is close by, and a hindrance is expected from him, then it is better to stop the ball in another way.

If the ball is stopped with the sole of the foot near an opponent, then an agile opponent will attack at the moment the ball is found under one foot and the body is balancing on the other foot. A little shove (the only kind allowed) would be quite enough to sever the player from the ball. Here a quicker, but more difficult way of stopping the ball can be used, namely, to stop and immediately take the ball along with the run. That can be done with the inside of the foot, or the outside by running up to the ball so that it bounces against the ground approximately one half meter behind the upper body. The inside of the foot is turned to the direction of the ball, with the knee slightly bent.

At the moment the ball bounces off the ground, it hits the inside of the foot and so loses its momentum. Now the foot is turned in the direction of the run and the ball is taken along. Stopping the ball and starting immediately are two separate activities that when joined save a lot of time. As with the inside of the foot, the outside can be used to stop the ball. Half high balls can be stopped with a lifted leg or with the body (the stomach, the chest).

In a training session, the following ways of stopping the ball must be practiced.

1. Stopping with the sole of the foot.
2. Stopping with the inside of the foot.
3. Stopping with the outside of the foot.
4. Stopping with a lifted foot (half high balls).
5. Stopping with the chest, stomach (half high balls).
6. Stopping with all kinds of possible maneuvers,
   with both shins,
   above the knees,

with the head, and
catching with the top of the foot.

Every good player is required to know how to stop the ball quickly and confidently. However, in the course of the game, it is often very important that the ball be passed onward by foot or head without stopping. That increases the tempo of the game and confuses the opponent. It is important to learn how to stop the ball while in motion.

A player will have completely mastered ball control when he wastes no unnecessary time when stopping the ball. Much is dependent on the way in which a player has positioned himself in the field. Every player, especially forwards, must know to never stand facing one's own goal. If the ball is expected from the back, one can turn back, but the body must always remain facing the opponent's goal, and in the worst case, facing parallel to the sidelines. If one must still turn when receiving the ball, in the first place time is lost, and in the second place, the player loses his overview of the field.

Dribbling means to outplay the opponent while maneuvering the ball with the feet. Dribbling is often exaggerated. The dribbler finds himself in a personal contest with one or more opponents. In order to be successful, he must fight his way through these opponents. It might be more convenient to pass the ball to a teammate. One must attempt to dribble straight ahead, not across the field or around in circles. Dribbling is used in every game, otherwise the game itself becomes too conventional. As I have already said, the need cannot be exaggerated.

In a game it is often tactically more correct to dribble. Forwards and halfbacks must have this tendency, but in no case should the fullbacks or goalies have it. The fullback may not dribble the ball, because by making even the slightest mistake, he might suffer consequences that are difficult to overcome. Tactically, it is sometimes very important to dribble the ball. However, dribblers can often be tactically poor players. If the ball comes to a one-sided dribbler, he usually battles until several opponents appear around him and then he loses the ball whether he wants to or not. Tactically, of course, nothing has come from this sort of dribbling. Dribbling may be done in the following instances:

1. if all teammates are covered
2. if teammates are in tactically inconvenient positions
3. in order to trick an opponent out of position
4. in order to surprise an opponent.

When dribbling, the player must have deft feet and good body technique. An important basic rule is not to try to outplay more than one opponent. Dribbling involves a big responsibility. In every case in which the team's safety is important, as in the case of fullbacks, the idea of dribbling must be dismissed. It is not worth outplaying the same opponent twice. The player who gives an outplayed opponent another chance to attack is making a great tactical error.

Outsmarting the opponent, along with technique and tactics, is an important part of the game of soccer. Outsmarting your opponent means convincing him of intentions that are, in effect, not your own. Just as boxers outsmart their opponents to surprise them with an unexpected hit, so soccer players make certain body movements to outsmart their opponents. It is enough to suddenly turn the head to one side so that the opponent's attention is distracted to that side for just a moment, and then to go right past him on the other side.

Dribbling the ball and outsmarting the opponent are often, but not always, performed simultaneously. The opponent can also be outsmarted without the ball. However, successful dribbling without outsmarting the opponent is almost impossible. It is easy to outsmart an opponent who is following by making a few upper body movements. The ball can be passed between the legs, it can be jumped over, or many different variations can occur, so that the opponent's attention is directed in the wrong direction. In general, outsmarting the opponent has many tactical advantages and it is also less risky than dribbling the ball.

Running with the ball. Running without the ball is the same as in running track, especially in the short-distance events. With the ball it is quite a different matter. Here it is important to move ahead with greater speed and without losing control of the ball.

That is why a player must know how to direct the ball well, otherwise it will go in a different direction from the one in which the player meant it to go. Besides that, while a player is running with the ball, the ball must be moved so that it takes away from the opponent's movements.

At every moment a player must be situated so that he is able to move, stop, or start in another direction. All this can be done only by moving with the ball, keeping it close to the body. When a player is running, his upper body usually leans forward; the ball can be found below it, and it is protected from attack.

A player must know how to move the ball just as well with the inside as the outside of the foot, and to move with the ball when running using short, quick steps so that direction can change at any moment.

The School of Running

The runs made by soccer players on the field earn special notice, because the flow is entirely different from that found in track and field.

For track athletes, running means conquering a set distance while going in a certain direction with a one-time exertion of energy. It is different for soccer players. They run quite a long distance, even several kilometers, throughout the entire soccer contest. The distance run is divided into numerous short sprints from five, ten, twenty to even forty meters, and, in addition, each of these sprints must be run at the greatest speed—that is to say that they must be run like a shot from a gun. Sometimes during the contest there are so-called moments of rest when the player is not running.

Actually, in a contest, soccer players don't really rest; they spend the entire game time making standing starts.

When sprinting, the greatest speed one can achieve depends on the first meters. These first meters are the deciding ones in the contest of soccer.

Furthermore, we see that the players suddenly change direction, confuse an opponent, or receive the ball.

All of this combined running, more correctly, sprinting, requires great endurance and energy from the player.

How then to gain endurance? Not by running a few laps around the field every practice day. The player who will have run such nonstop, long distances during practice will wonder why during the contest he will easily tire and why he will be the one who always gets to the ball later than the player who has practiced the proper training methods.

Therefore, let's do away with this long-distance training, which until now is and has been used! The correct endurance training will occur if players run the aforementioned long distances with breaks—more correctly—as sprints with breaks.

These sprints must be alternatively from five to thirty meters long. Once every two or three weeks, a few 200-meter runs, and even less frequently 400-meter runs can be utilized. Besides these runs, a standing start, a change in direction, and a sprint around and through obstacles must be practiced.

By training to run in such a way, the players will gain both speed and endurance.

Body Development (Calisthenics)

Body development uses all kinds of games such as children use in school. Volleyball and basketball are very useful here. The most important, though, are calisthenics with and without equipment. Calisthenics cannot be lacking in any soccer practice.

Lessons for All Players

The art of soccer: control of the ball and body. Taking and covering an open position. Congeniality and the drive in a contest. Complete knowledge of short and long, precise passes. A rich use and manipulation of soccer's ideas and plays. Wing forwards' and halfbacks' teamwork is very important.

When near your own goal: play calmly, quickly, thoughtfully, being wary of the opponent's every step. Take away all chances for the opponent to work freely. Don't allow him to take a shot at the goal. Get the ball away from the goal as soon as possible. Pass to the halfback or even the goalie if there is no other choice. Also, always stop the opponent while facing him.

In the middle of the field: confident and precise building of the game. Backward passing can also be useful. When possible, quickly taking the ball to the opponent's goal. Preparing the situation for a kick to the goal and the gaining of a goal.

At the opponent's goal: do not delay. Cold-bloodedly and quickly find an open position. Pass precisely, at just the right moment. Shoot, shoot, and shoot again.

Free kicks and throw-ins: quickly take positions. Quickly make the kick or throw before the opponent can cover. On your side of the field, a free kick is made by the fullback or center halfback, but on the opponent's side, by the halfback. If possible, shoot directly towards the opponent's goal to the team's best shooter.

Never leave: an opponent who is moving away with the ball or who is trying to take an open position. Do not leave if the ball is imprecisely passed and when a shot is made at the opponent's goal.

When hitting a ball out of the goal, always try to pass to an open teammate. Usually, in these instances, the wing forwards go far back to receive these passes. In this instance, the halfbacks must watch the opponent's forwards.

After making an eleven-meter penalty kick, one player from each team must go toward the goal, so that in case the ball bounces off the goalie, it can be sent back toward the goal. In the same manner, two of the defenders must hinder these repeated attempts. Just do not run too quickly or too late.

Tactics have one principle: in the deciding moment—complete confidence. Do not allow one and the same opponent to attack you twice in a row. Take an open position quickly and intelligently and play the ball in time. When dribbling the ball, the body must be between the ball and the opponent.

If possible, don't let high balls bounce, but stop them when they first touch the ground, because otherwise the opponent has time to attack and an unnecessary fight for the ball occurs.

Never turn your back to the contest. Always watch the ball, opposing players, teammates, and the entire game.

Fight calmly, but not slowly.

You must let the ball and the opponent run, and you must also run without the ball.

The game goes two times forty-five minutes. Only then does the contest end. Don't rest on your laurels before then, because the opponent can regain what he has lost and can even win.

The game ends in just ninety minutes. Make goals in time!

A very important phrase in soccer is—"in time!"

Types of Soccer Games

The beginning period of soccer (for us in Latvia as well) was famous for players' individual performances. It is possible that in earlier times, there were many more dribbling artists than there are now. One must think that these people knew little of tactics, but rather, gave all their attention to ball technique. As the game slowly developed, a smoother kind of contest play was used and certain kinds of tactics appeared. Without a doubt, the use of plays, as compared to the earlier game, was a big achievement.

The Scots were the first to start to use short, low plays in the game, which is why even now this type of game is called the "Scots' style."

The ball must do its job. That is at the foundation of soccer. The ball does not tire and reaches its goal more quickly than the quickest player. Before the "Scots' style" appeared, the so-called "kick and rush" style was known. In translation, that would be the "hit and run." Here (in the contest with the opponent), the ball is hit whenever possible to the opponent's goal and, while running, one tries to stop it. This style is entirely primitive. Very often the game became a beating of the ball without a plan, besides which, the game also lost much of its beauty, because the players' power and speed was exaggerated.

The new style then developed in Scotland, where as in chess, the ball was pushed here and there with the goal of outplaying, tiring, and beating the opponent through a series of passes. This "Scot's style" has its bad side, which is that if the contest takes place on a small or uneven field, then often these chess moves aren't successful. Besides that, players can get carried away with passing the ball (they overplay) and lose a lot of time. With time, the Scots saw their style's faults and started to correct them. With this, the modern style of play has developed. This is such that short and long passes are interchanged and players take the shortest route to the opponent's goal, which is followed by sharp shots at the goal.

The Spectators

The sport of soccer progresses each year; the number of players grows, and the spectators multiply. But do they have a general knowledge of the rules of the game of soccer? The lack of knowledge of even the most basic rules is proven by their frequent dissatisfaction with the officials and the players. This is not becoming to the spectators.

Dear spectator, do you know that the player is positioned behind the ball at the moment he passes it, not when he receives it? Does every spectator also know that purposely touching the ball with a hand is penalized? How poor is the knowledge about pushing an opponent (blocking with the body)! A player is allowed to strongly push the opponent (not with the hands), but the rules say that the player cannot be harmed by the push. Sometimes we don't even break the rules' boundaries if the opponent does a small somersault in mid-air, or if he is pushed precisely at the moment when he is on one foot with the other foot raised for a kick. On a corner kick or throw-in from the sideline, no one is offsides. Do you think everyone knows this? But once a third player touches the ball, offsides occurs.

In this case, doesn't the official, who is closest to the point of play, see infractions of the rules better and more quickly than the spectator who is on the side of the field, and often far back in the stands? The official is found between both teams' players and can see every small infraction that occurs near the goal, often in a crowd, very well. If the official suddenly blows his whistle and points to the eleven-meter line, then the spectator, who has more sympathy for the suffering team, loudly lays the blame on the official. This is not right from the point of view of the spectator. The official must penalize every infraction, regardless of whether it occurs in the penalty area or elsewhere. There are many other instances when the spectator will not agree with the official.

As I already said, most spectators do not know the rules of soccer, and so it would be better not to disturb the official. Courses are arranged for our officials in which knowledge of the rules is taught and expanded; therefore, one must think that in the future they will make fewer mistakes. From my heart, I would like to encourage all spectators to do all that is possible to become familiar with the rules of the game of soccer. Then disagreements will not occur, and the game itself will seem more captivating and interesting.

A Short List of Rules of Play

No more than eleven players may play on each side in the game of soccer. On the basis of a common agreement, some players may be interchanged.

The playing field is marked by lines, which on the sides or sidelines are 90 to 120 meters. The width, end lines—45 to 90 meters. In the middle of the field, from one sideline to the other, a line is drawn that divides the field into two equal parts.

The middle of the field is marked with a circle whose diameter is 9.15 meters.

The goals are marked with two vertical poles that are placed on the end line at an equal distance from the corner flags with a 7.32 meter distance between them. They are joined by a cross pole 2.44 meters high. Goal posts may not be more than 12.5 centimeters wide. 5.5 meters from each goalpost, a perpendicular line is drawn, a 5.5-meter-long line, which, when the ends are joined, forms the so-called 5.5 area (the goal area). The same kind of lines are drawn at a distance of 16.5 meters from the goal posts and end lines. This part of the field is called the penalty area.

In the middle of the goal area, at a distance of 11 meters, a spot is drawn from which 11-meter penalty kicks are made.

Taking the 11-meter spot as the center, outside the penalty area part of a circle is drawn whose diameter is 9.15 meters.

The circumference of the ball may not be greater than 68.5 centimeters and not less than 71 centimeters. In international play, a field 100-110 meters long and 65-75 meters wide is used.

At the beginning of the game, the ball may weigh 396 to 453 grams.

stura miets = corner post
vartu linija = goal line
varti = goal
vartu laukums = goal area
soda laukums = penalty area
soda punkts = penalty spot
sanu linija = sideline
aplis = center circle
pusloks = center half circle
vidus linija = midfield line

1. The game lasts ninety minutes (if there is no agreement to the contrary). Possession of the ball at the beginning of the game and sides of the field are chosen by lot. The game begins from the middle of the field and the ball must be passed to the opponent's side of the field. At that moment, the opponent may not be closer than 9.15 meters from the ball.
2. The teams change sides of the field at halftime. After the first forty-five minutes, the contest is stopped for five to fifteen minutes. In the second half, play is begun by the team that lost the draw at the beginning of the first half. After a goal, play is started from the center by the team that lost the goal, just as in the beginning of the game.
3. A goal is considered made if the ball has gone past the goal posts and crossbar. It cannot be thrown in with the hands, but must be headed or kicked in by the attacking

team's players. The team that gains the most goals, wins. If in the entire game no goals are made, or if the score is even, then the game is undecided.

The ball remains in the field of play if it bounces off the goal posts, corner flag posts, the official or side judge if he is on the field.

The ball is considered out of the field as soon as it has completely crossed the side or end line in the air or on the ground.

4. If the ball has crossed the sideline, then it is thrown in from the point where it left the field by a player on the team that did not send it out of play. When making a throw-in, the player must stand on both feet on or outside the sideline, facing the field. The ball must be thrown in with both hands over the head. The ball is in play as soon as it is thrown into the field. If the throw-in rules are broken, then the throw-in is done by the opposing team. A goal directly from a throw-in is not counted. The player who throws in the ball may not touch it until another one of the players has touched it. If the rule is broken, the opponent gets a free kick.
5. If a player has the ball then every one of his teammates, who at that moment is closer to the opponent's goal line than to the ball is offsides and may not participate in play or in any way hinder the opponent's play, except in the case in which two opponents are found closer to their own goal line. The player is not offsides in cases of rebounds from the goal, corner kick, throw-ins from the sidelines if the last player to touch the ball was one of the opponents, or also if the player receiving the ball is on his own side of the field.
6. If a player from the attacking team hits the ball over the opponent's end line, then the ball is hit from the goal by one of the opposing team's players. A kick from the goal

must go at least over the penalty area's line. The kick is made from the end line in the area closest to the place where the ball went out of the field. If the ball is hit across a player's own end line, a corner kick follows, which is made by a member of the opposing team. A corner kick is made from the 1-meter mark found in the corner closest to the point where the ball went out of the field. The player making the corner kick may not play the ball again until another player has touched it.

When a corner kick is being made, opponents may not be closer than 9.15 meters.

7. The goalie, while in his own team's penalty area, may move forward with the ball in his hands but not more than two steps. On the third step, he must kick the ball or let it fall to the ground, then he can go forward two steps after picking it up again.

   The goalie may be pushed if he has the ball in his hands, if he is hindering the opponent, and if he has left the goal area. Another player may be substituted for the goalie by telling the official beforehand.

8. Any kind of rudeness which might be associated with bad luck is forbidden.

   All players, except the goalie in his own penalty area, are forbidden to purposely touch the ball with their hands. The hands may also not be used to hold or push an opponent.

   The opponent may be pushed with the body, not too sharply or rudely. A player may not be pushed from the back, except if he is purposely hindering his opponent.

9. When making free kicks, an opponent may be no closer than 9.15 meters from the ball, except if the opponent is on his own end line between the goal posts. The player making the free kick may not touch the ball a second

time until another player has touched it. After a free kick, the ball is considered in play only if it has made one rotation or has rolled the distance of its circumference.

10. A goal can be made directly from a corner kick. If a free kick is given for a paragraph 9 violation, then it can also be made for a goal, but goals cannot be made directly from other kicks.
11. The player's cleats may not have sharp nail points. In the same vein, shin guards may not have some sort of metal parts. Extra soles on the shoes (cork) or leather stripes may not be higher or wider than 12 millimeters. The extra soles may not be conical, but must average 12 millimeters. A player whose shoes do not meet the above requirements is to be sent off the field by the official. He may return to the field only when the ball is outside the field, and, he must show himself to the official, and the official must check the uniform of said player. The official may check uniforms at the beginning of the game, as well as at halftime.
12. The officials' assignment is to keep the flow of the game going within the parameters of the rules. When the rules are purposely broken, the official must give a warning to the violator, and must give the opposing team a free kick. If a penalty is repeated, as well as if a rule is broken vulgarly, the official may send the player off the field without a warning.
13. There are two line judges whose assignment is to decide if the ball is across the sideline and which team gets the corner kick or throw-in. They must also help the official keep the game within the parameters of the rules. If the sideline judge interferes with the judge's exercise of competence too often, the official has the right to send him off the field and to name someone else in his place.
14. If the official has stopped the game without an infraction

of the rules, he lets the ball fall to the ground at the place where it was at the moment play was stopped. In these cases, the ball is considered in play only if it has touched the ground.

15. If the rules in paragraphs 6, 8, and 10 are broken, or a player is given a warning and sent off the field, according to paragraph 13, the official must give a free kick from the point where the infraction took place.

If the infractions in paragraph 9 are made outside the penalty area, then the official must give the free kick from the place where the infraction occurred. On the other hand, if the infraction occurs inside the penalty area, an eleven-meter penalty kick must be given.

On an eleven-meter penalty kick, all the players, except the player making the kick and the opposing goalie, must be in the field, but outside the penalty area, and no closer than 9.15 meters from the eleven-meter point.

A goal may be gained directly from these kinds of kicks. The player making the penalty kick may not hit the ball a second time until another player has touched it. If a goal is gained on an eleven-meter penalty kick, but a player on the defending team has committed a violation, then the violation is not taken into account.

The Latvia Cup

A regular cup tournament was already held in the very first years of our soccer activities. The Latvian Soccer Federation even created a cup, which was fought for by all of Latvia's teams, and which was named the Latvia Cup. However, the battle for the cup was completely overshadowed in comparison to the national championship tournament, and gained only little popularity.

The year 1937 was a historic year for the Latvia Cup tournament, when, with the help of our country's "first citizen," the president, Karlis Ulmanis, the cup tournament order was completely reorganized. Our people's leader gave a wonderfully beautiful, massive, traveling cup, the Latvia Cup. The Latvian Federation of Soccer designed special rules for the competition for the cup, which stipulated that all of Latvia's registered teams would be required to start in the tournament. In the past two years, the Cup games have been received with great enthusiasm and celebration, even in the farthest reaches of Latvia. Interest in the results of the Cup tournament has become huge, because all teams which have any say in Latvia's soccer community are in the ranks of the tournament. Up to now, the renewed Latvia Cup has been won twice and has been won by:

RFK in 1937
The Riga Wolves in 1938

The Latvia Cup is truly a unifying element in the community of soccer, because only in this tournament do all of Latvia's teams meet in an equal environment.

Not Eleven Men, but One Team

In soccer, one single player does not compete with another single player, but rather, a team matches forces with another team. For this reason, a player's individual skills are not as important as all eleven men's teamwork. How many countless times has it been heard that an "all-star" team is beaten by a virtually unrecognized and unknown opponent. And only when one starts to find out more about the "unknowns" does a familiar scene unfold. The favorites have been outplayed by a team that for years has trustfully played together, whose players know each other almost better than they know themselves. They—eleven men have fought against individual success and have won as a team. Many readers probably will have heard of the classical land of sport, where soccer is especially well regarded. Thousands of players—professionals—earn their "daily bread" competing in the soccer field. They have no other job than soccer.

In England, there is a frequent buying of excellent players, where the case is not rare, that large sums change hands. It is not uncommon that this money is spent in vain. The bought soccer player certainly does play brilliantly, and does not play as an individual until he comes to an understanding with his fellow contestants. Then, when a break comes, the closely welded team no longer works on the field but is divided. In soccer, in the end, the most important thing is not to play well. The first priority should be that you can have an understanding with others—and by keeping this most precious characteristic in mind, even the individually less outstanding player meets such challenges, that even eleven of his country's best armed men cannot do.

In reality, in soccer it is very wrong to laud individual players, because what would they have done if their ideas had not been supported by the other ten contestants? Without a doubt, the ten would more easily get by without the one, than the one without the ten. Of course, people are not all created with the same vision and even less with the same character, but they are all given the characteristic of impatience—to search for the best and the strongest. It happens this way in team sports—soccer, where someone is always trying to "fish out" from the group the most unconquerable. Only one question is always clear: is the one who is most lauded the one who gave the most to the whole team's working together?

And often the truth, which sometimes is never made public, can be that the menial labor has been done by someone else, and this has gone unnoticed and unmarveled at by anyone. And this kind of "eleven unnoticed fighters" would be an ideal supplement to soccer. **On the field, the team must shine**—not the individual player—all the players with the same color of uniform. The world need not know what their names are—Sindelars, Drakes, Braines, Zamorrs, or maybe otherwise, but everyone should know the name earned by their unconquerable union, the outstanding results of their unselfishly working together. Of course, this ideal will always remain an ideal, **but every day in the future, just as the past and the present, will tell of one team's, not eleven players' superiority.**

The Balance Sheet for the Latvian National Team in Seventeen Years (1922–1939)

The Latvian all-star soccer team first made its debut as the national team on September 24, 1922. Our opponent in this historic contest was our northern neighbor—Estonia. This contest ended in a tie of 1-1. At the start of 1939, seventeen seasons had already passed since this most notable event, in which time Latvian soccer and its most outstanding players—the national team players—had experienced many things. There had been many days filled with happiness, but many times had been just as sad. If we looked over the "balance sheet," of the seventeen summers, we could be totally satisfied—we had more wins than losses in national competitions. **These years showed a positive evaluation for Latvian soccer.** Here are listed all of the Latvian national team's games and our opponents, and, most importantly, the results of the contests. (Latvia's team score is always listed first.)

Latvia—Estonia

September 24, 1922 in Riga	1-1
July 24, 1923 in Tallinn	1-1
October 18, 1924 in Riga	2-0
August 26, 1925 in Tallinn	2-2
September 19, 1926 in Riga	0-1
June 16, 1927 in Tallinn	1-4
September 25, 1927 in Riga	4-1

Latvia—Estonia

July 27, 1928 in Tallinn	1-0
September 23, 1928 in Riga	1-1
August 16, 1929 in Riga	2-2
September 18, 1929 in Tallinn	1-4
June 27, 1930 in Tallinn	1-1
August 16, 1930 in Kaunas	3-2
May 28, 1931 in Riga	0-1
September 1, 1931 in Tallinn	1-3
September 27, 1931 in Riga	2-1
July 1, 1932 in Tallinn	0-3
August 30, 1932 in Riga	1-0
May 28, 1933 in Riga	2-0
August 9, 1933 in Tallinn	1-2
September 3, 1933 in Kaunas	1-0
June 12, 1935 in Riga	1-1
August 22, 1935 in Tallinn	1-1
May 28, 1936 in Tallinn	4-3
August 31, 1936 in Riga	2-1
September 4, 1937 in Kaunas	1-1
September 7, 1937 in Kaunas	2-0
September 19, 1937 in Riga	3-1
July 20, 1938 in Tallinn	2-0
September 5, 1938 in Tallinn	1-1

In 30 games, Latvia had 13 wins, 7 losses, and 10 ties.

Latvia—Lithuania

July 6, 1924 in Kaunas	4-2
September 20, 1925 in Riga	2-2
August 21, 1926 in Kaunas	3-2
July 27, 1927 in Riga	6-3
July 25, 1928 in Tallinn	3-0
September 1, 1928 in Kaunas	1-1
August 14, 1929 in Riga	3-1
August 17, 1930 in Kaunas	3-3
July 30, 1931 in Riga	5-2
August 31, 1931 in Tallinn	1-0
June 29, 1932 in Kaunas	2-1
July 24, 1932 in Liepaja	2-1
August 28, 1932 in Kaunas	4-1

Latvia—Lithuania

September 11, 1932 in Kaunas	0-1
June 12, 1933 in Riga	6-2
September 4, 1933 in Kaunas	2-2
June 10, 1934 in Kaunas	0-2
September 9, 1934 in Riga	1-3
May 31, 1935 in Riga	6-1
August 21, 1935 in Tallinn	2-2
September 8, 1935 in Kaunas	2-2
June 14, 1936 in Kaunas	5-1
August 29, 1936 in Riga	2-1
June 29, 1937 in Riga	4-2
September 3, 1937 in Kaunas	5-1
May 17, 1938 in Riga	2-0
September 4, 1938 in Tallinn	1-1

In 27 games, Latvia had 17 wins, 3 losses, and 7 ties.

Latvia—Sweden

July 20, 1926 in Riga	4-1
May 29, 1927 in Stockholm	0-12
July 6, 1928 in Riga	0-4
July 28, 1929 in Malmo	0-10
July 22, 1930 in Riga	0-5
July 26, 1931 in Vesteross	0-6
July 13, 1932 in Riga	0-0
July 4, 1933 in Riga	1-1
September 23, 1934 in Stockholm	1-3
July 5, 1935 in Riga	0-3
June 10, 1938 in Stockholm	3-3

In 11 games, Latvia had 1 win, 7 losses, and 3 ties.

Latvia—Finland

August 13, 1924 in Riga	0-2
August 9, 1925 in Helsinki	1-3
August 12, 1926 in Riga	1-4
September 11, 1927 in Helsinki	1-3
September 19, 1928 in Riga	2-1
September 15, 1929 in Helsinki	1-3

Latvia—Finland

August 4, 1930 in Riga	3-0
August 19, 1931 in Helsinki	0-4
August 14, 1934 in Riga	1-1
June 6, 1935 in Helsinki	1-4

In 10 games, Latvia had 2 wins, 7 losses, and 1 tie.

Latvia—Poland

October 26, 1930 in Warsaw	0-6
July 5, 1931 in Riga	0-5
October 2, 1932 in Warsaw	1-2
October 14, 1934 in Riga	2-6
September 15, 1935 in Lodz	3-3
September 6, 1936 in Riga	3-3
October 10, 1937 in Katowice	1-2
September 25, 1938 in Riga	2-1

In 8 games, Latvia had 1 win, 5 losses, and 2 ties.

Latvia—Germany

October 13, 1935 in Koningsberg	0-3
June 25, 1937 in Riga	1-3

In 2 games, Latvia had 2 losses.

Latvia—France

May 27, 1924 in Paris	0-7

In 1 game, Latvia had 1 loss.

Latvia—Turkey

June 22, 1924 in Riga	1-3

In 1 game, Latvia had 1 loss.

Latvia—Romania

July 12, 1937 in Riga	0-0

In 1 game, there was 1 tie.

Latvia—Austria

September 5, 1937 in Vienna 1-2

In 1 game, Latvia had 1 loss.

Latvia—Hungary

June 28, 1938 in Riga 3-0

In 1 game, Latvia had 1 win.

Latvia—Czechoslovakia

August 28, 1938 in Riga 2-1

In 1 game, Latvia had 1 win.

It is especially pleasant to discern that Latvian soccer has truly done well in the recent past. The climax was 1938 **when our national team did not lose a single game,** even though our opponents were big soccer countries such as Hungary, Czechoslovakia, and Sweden. In seventeen years, Latvian soccer completed 94 national games, in which it gained 36 wins, experienced 34 losses, and 24 games have ended in ties. Therefore, our wins outnumbered our losses by 2. It was also interesting to note that since 1934, against our closest neighbors and most frequent opponents—Estonia and Lithuania—we lost not a single national game—there were only wins and some tie games.